Donkey runs away.

What now?

'I can sing with friends.'

'Can you sing, dog?'

'Woof-woof!'

'Can you sing, cat?'

'Miaow-miaow!'

'Can you sing, cock?'

'Cock-a-doodle-do!'

'Let's sing in Bremen.'

6

Night falls.
'We're hungry!'

'There!'

'A house!'

'Food! Beds!'

'Cock-a-doodle-do!'

'Look!'
'Robbers!'
'Let's sing!'

'Miaow!'

'Woof!'

'Eeyore!'

9

The robbers run away.

The animals are happy.

Food!

One robber
comes again.

'Help!'

'Big monsters!'
'Big teeth!'
'Run!'

'Let's live here forever.'

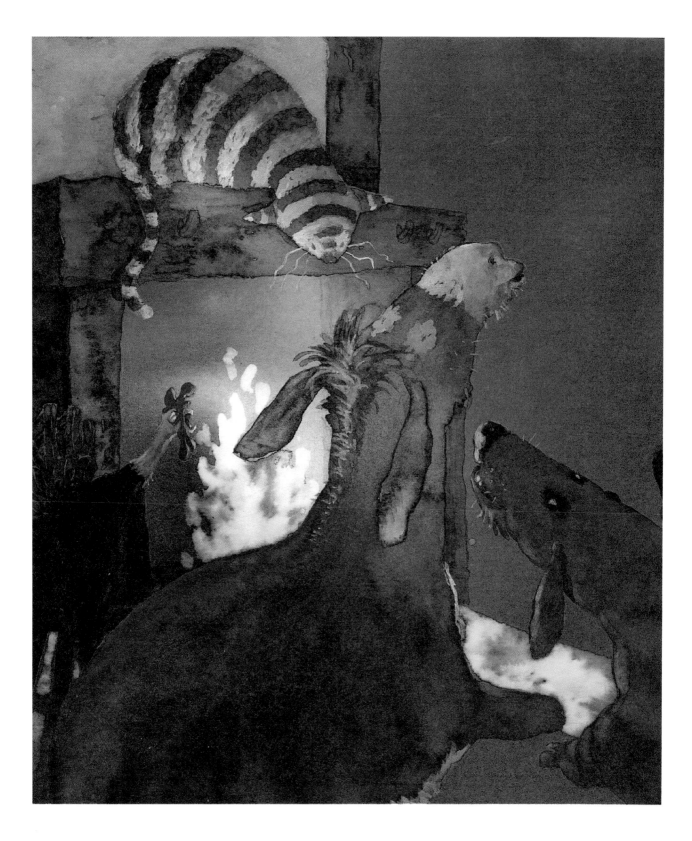

ACTIVITIES

BEFORE YOU READ

1. Look at the picture on the front of the book.

    a) Yes ✔ or no ✘ ?
        ☐ There are 2 animals.
        ☐ There are 4 animals.
        ☐ There are 6 animals.

    b) Yes ✔ or no ✘ ?
        The animals are...

        ☐   ☐   ☐   ☐   ☐   ☐

    c) Yes ✔ or no ✘ ?
        The animals are...   ☐ smiling   ☐ eating
                               ☐ singing   ☐ playing

AFTER YOU READ

2. Can you match these?

    Cock-a-doodle-do   cock

    miaow-miaow   donkey

    woof-woof   cat

    eeyore   dog

Pearson Education Limited
Edinburgh Gate, Harlow
Essex CM20 2JE, England
and Associated Companies throughout the world.

ISBN 0582 344034

First published by Librairie du Liban Publishers, 1996
This adaptation first published 2000 under licence by Penguin Books
© 2000 Penguin Books Limited
Illustrations © 1996 Librairie du Liban

1 3 5 7 9 10 8 6 4 2

Series Editors: Annie Hughes and Melanie Williams
The Musicians of Bremen, Level 1, Retold by Simon Smith

Designed by Shireen Nathoo Design
Illustrations by Odilon Moraes

Printed in Scotland by Scotprint, Musselburgh

Published by Pearson Education Limited in association with Penguin Books Ltd,
both companies being subsidiaries of Pearson Plc

For a complete list of the title available in the Penguin Young Readers series please write to your
local Pearson education office or to: Marketing Department, Penguin Longman Publishing,
5 Bentinck Street, London W1M 5RN